A Moment to Reflect

Letting Go

Meditations for Codependents

HAZELDEN

1817

A Harper/Hazelden Book

Harper & Row, Publishers, San Francisco

New York, Grand Rapids, Philadelphia, St. Louis
London, Singapore, Sydney, Tokyo, Toronto

FIRST HARPER & ROW EDITION PUBLISHED IN 1989.

Library of Congress Catalog Card Number: 89–45619
ISBN 0-06-255402-6

89 90 91 92 93 SEXTON 10 9 8 7 6 5 4 3 2 1

INTRODUCTION

Concentrating our energies on that which is within our power and responsibility to control, and letting go of everything else, makes our behavior more positive and effective. We stop wasting time and energy, stop making ourselves frustrated and miserable. We start taking care of ourselves in the truest and best sense.

—Veronica Ray
  Letting Go of Control
  Hazelden Audio Cassette Series

The meditations within are dedicated to the important, often difficult task of releasing our old self-defeating attitudes and behaviors. We can move forward toward greater peace and serenity by letting go of the past and the future; obsessions with other people's feelings and problems; old guilt, shame, fear, and pain; destructive relationships; impatience; perfectionism; fearfulness; pessimism; and magical thinking.

Letting go frees us to live in the present and build a better future. Without the weight of our old patterns holding us back, we can move forward along our path of spiritual growth. We can reach for new, healthier, happier ways of living.

Now we face all of our old self-defeating attitudes and behaviors, recognize and release them. We take the time and energy needed to discover and let go of everything within that's been keeping us from happiness and well-being.

Letting go may frighten us at first, until we discover its liberating effects in our lives. As Veronica Ray wrote in *A Design for Growth*, "It's like learning to swim. If we thrash about in the water, tense and fearful, we'll sink as surely as a stone. But if we completely relax and let go, the water will lift us up and we'll float. We can now relax into the flow of the river of life, trusting our Higher Power to take care of us."

Accepting Help

We are learning to take care of ourselves, to be more independent, and to trust ourselves and our Higher Power. But this doesn't mean we have to do everything alone. We can ask for and accept the help we need from others.

Sometimes we need to talk and someone can help us by listening. Sometimes we need the information or experience that another person can share with us. Sometimes we need to laugh, play, or just be with other people. There are many healthy ways people can help each other.

When we let go of our belief that we have to do it all alone, we become open to receiving help from others. Sometimes our Higher Power reaches out to us through them. No one can live our lives or solve our problems for us, but we can let go of our fears and mistrust, and accept the help we need.

I let go of my fear of accepting help when I need it.

Guilt

Of all our judgments against people, our harshest are probably those against ourselves. We replay in our minds every mistake, failure, and regrettable incident. We may quickly forget our moments of love, kindness, generosity, and success.

Harboring guilt over our past misdeeds only harms us and others. It keeps us from facing the present with a positive attitude. It feeds our low self-esteem and hopelessness. Once an event slips away into the past, there is nothing anyone can do to get it back. We can either cling to its memory or let it go.

In the past, we did the best we could. Now we can do better. We can concentrate on the present. We can focus on avoiding mistakes and immediately rectifying those that do occur. We can move ever forward, free of the chains of old, useless guilt.

I now release all of my old guilt and forgive myself for all of my past mistakes.

Worry

As codependents, we often spend a great deal of time worrying about others. This may not appear to be destructive, because it's something we do in our minds. But it has destructive effects for two reasons.

First, never in the course of human history has worrying solved a problem. It only fills us with negative thoughts.

Second, it robs us of the time and energy we need to use positively. With our attention focused on worrying, we can't fully be wherever we are at any given time. We can't concentrate on the things we can and should do something about. Worry distracts us from the real business of living.

Letting go of worry is a choice we can make. We can refuse to turn over our minds to anxiety and fear. We are powerless over others, but not over our own thoughts.

I let go of worrying about people and things I can't control.

Self-Will Versus God's Will

What is our self-will? Does it guide us to health and happiness? Is it based on our own best interests? What is God's will for us? Where does it lead us?

These can be confusing questions we ask ourselves as we develop spiritually. We all want to be happy, to think and act in ways that enhance our well-being. But often we don't know what our best interests really are. This causes our self-defeating behavior. This is our ego's self-will.

God's will is always for our highest good. Our ego may allow us to do things that harm others. It may convince us that our happiness lies in acquiring possessions or finding the right relationship. But our Higher Power knows that destructive behavior toward anyone harms us, and that our happiness and well-being come from within ourselves. God's will is our own true will.

I let go of my ego's self-will, and God shows me my true will for happiness and well-being.

Forgiveness

Hanging on to our grievances against others may make us feel safe. We may believe that letting go of them will make us vulnerable to attack. We may fear appearing weak.

But our grievances keep us from happiness. They bind us to positions of attack or defense. They hold us down to misery and pain. They rob us of our spiritual strengths.

Letting go of our grievances toward others and the world frees us from our distractions and obstacles to finding happiness. Forgiveness allows us to move forward on our spiritual path. Forgiveness opens our minds and hearts to new ways of seeing others, the world, and ourselves. Forgiveness opens us up to our Higher Power's guidance and help.

I let go of all my grievances against others.

Unlearning Old Habits

As we move forward in our lives, and learn new ways of living, we may have to unlearn some old patterns of thinking and behaving. Letting go of familiar ways of seeing the world can be a little frightening. Familiarity may give us the illusion of safety, even when we know it's actually self-defeating.

With trust in our Higher Power, we can make an effort to replace our old habits with new, healthier ones. It can be like moving to a place where people drive on the other side of the street. It may feel a little strange for a while, but we can get used to it. Clinging stubbornly to our old ways of driving would only cause us trouble and could result in serious damage.

We can let go of our old familiar ways, and let our Higher Power guide us to new lives.

I now let go of all my old, self-defeating habits.

Saying Good-bye

Letting go of a relationship may be hard for us if we've forgotten who we were outside of it. We may have thought of ourselves as someone's wife, husband, lover, friend, parent, or child. Letting go may be our chance to discover who we are simply as *someone.*

Whether or not the relationship ended by our own choice can also affect our reaction. It may be easier to let go of a relationship that we feel is detrimental to our well-being. But when the decision is not ours, we may cling to our pain a little longer.

When we turn to our Higher Power in trust, we can say good-bye to the relationship, knowing its ending is for the best. Letting go of our pain frees us to accept the new joys God has in store for us.

I release my pain and trust my Higher Power's will for me.

Optimism

It may be hard for us to let go of other people and their problems if we fear terrible things will happen, or if we feel our worry and interference are holding another person's life together.

But if we trust our Higher Power, we can begin to assume that all will be well. We can let go, knowing that whatever happens will be God's will. We can accept that God knows better than we do.

We may say we trust God, but we don't trust other people. But what others choose to do is not our responsibility. It is between them and their Higher Power. We are only trying to control things we can never control when we worry about them. Optimism means letting go of worry about the future. The future is in God's hands, and there's no better place for it to be.

Today I will expect all to be well in God's care.

Accepting Tragedy

No matter who we are or where we are on our path, tragedy can strike us or our loved ones. As Leo Buscaglia says, "We cannot stop a hurricane, silence a storm, or keep a loved one from leaving us." These things, and others, just happen.

It may be hard for us to understand why God allows tragedies to occur. We may feel betrayed. We may want to give up on God or this whole spirituality business. We may wonder why we should bother working so hard at our spiritual growth, only to be ignored in our time of need.

But after our grief and our anger, we can experience another feeling: acceptance. God has wisdom and a plan we know nothing about. Letting go means accepting both the painful and the joyful gifts our Higher Power sends us.

I accept life's tragedies with serenity.

Turn It Over

Controlling behavior may give us the illusion of security. But we will always be safer in the hands of God than under the rule of our self-will. God doesn't make mistakes or lead us into destructive behavior.

People, relationships, and situations do not need us to run them. We only make ourselves and others unhappy by insisting that they do. When we accept our true powerlessness and turn all of these things over to our Higher Power, we find they sort themselves out. Even if people don't make the choices we would have them make, we can let go and accept it.

We can remember to ask God to take over everything and to give us the serenity to accept His will. Our true security lies in accepting God's will over our own.

I let go of all of my controlling thoughts and behaviors, and God takes care of me.

Letting God

Trusting our Higher Power helps us to let go of controlling thoughts and behaviors. We can't choose what's best for others. Only God can do that. When we let go, we can remember that whatever happens is in God's hands.

We may be tempted to judge others, but we can stop ourselves by remembering to trust our Higher Power. We can accept that we don't understand everything, and we don't have to. We can let God take over.

"Letting God" means letting go of our judgments. It is not up to us to involve ourselves in others' problems and choices. That's not why we're here. Whatever happens in other people's lives is between them and their Higher Power. We can concentrate on our own lives and responsibilities, our own growth and spirituality. That's enough for each of us to handle.

I trust God to take over all the things I've tried to control.

Today's Lesson

When we are obsessed with other people's lives and problems, we miss everything else that's going on. Every day God sends us messages and lessons to be learned. But we can't see them if our minds are focused elsewhere.

No one else can learn our lessons for us, and we can't learn anyone else's for them. They are tailor-made for each of us. Our Higher Power finds ways to present our particular lessons in our lives. Only by letting go of being overly involved in others' lives can we receive the message God has for us.

We can't control others, and focusing on them only stops us from learning what we can today. Instead, we can accept that others have their lessons to learn and we have ours.

Today God has a lesson for me that is for no one else. I am open to receiving His guidance.

Choosing Happiness

Ironically, the more we try to control others, the more we are controlled. Our emotions become reactions to others rather than reflecting true choices. Happiness, to us, becomes no more than fleeting moments of relief tied to the moods and behaviors of others.

Happiness is a choice. We can choose to let go of attempts to control people, relationships, and situations, and thereby free ourselves from their control. We can choose to let go of anger and resentment when others don't fulfill our expectations. We can choose to live our own lives and work on our own growth.

Happiness isn't having everyone and everything go our way. It grows out of a quiet choice to accept the things we can't control and to concentrate on changing what we can—ourselves.

I choose happiness by acting on my own behalf rather than reacting to others.

Caretaking

In some of our relationships, we may have taken over decisions and responsibilities for others. We may have lied or covered up for others, removed the consequences of their choices, or overwhelmed them with unwelcome advice.

Letting go of these behaviors may seem irresponsible to us. We may believe others can't get along without our help. We may feel certain the world will come tumbling down on them if we let go.

Maybe we can make better decisions than someone else, but *it doesn't matter.* It's not our responsibility to get involved in other people's decisions or problems. Though they make mistakes, we must not make their choices for them.

Letting go and letting God take over others' problems frees us to take care of our own. And even with God's help, that's all we can truly handle.

I trust God to help others take care of themselves.

Material Loss

Material things come and go. They break, wear out, get lost, and lose their usefulness. Fashions and individual tastes change. Money is earned and spent. Nothing material lasts forever.

Nevertheless, when we lose something we value, we may become upset. We may feel a sense of insecurity or vulnerability. But losing something can teach us we really don't need it at all.

In fact, we can survive quite comfortably with very little. The quality of our lives isn't created outside ourselves. It comes from a healthy self-image, serenity, and our relationship with our Higher Power.

We can accept material loss as a valuable lesson. When we concentrate our attention on spiritual growth, we discover that we can be perfectly safe and happy, with or without material things.

I am perfectly fine, even when I lose material things.

Word Power

If we listened to a tape recording of everything we said in a day, we'd probably be surprised. We might hear a lot of negative words like *can't, won't, don't, couldn't,* and *shouldn't.* We might hear ourselves vehemently declare "I hate. . ." several times.

Becoming aware of the negative words we use can help us recognize our negative thoughts. We may think we have faith in positive change and feel optimistic about the future, but we use words like *can't, always, never,* and *impossible.* We may not think we harbor angry or resentful thoughts, but our speech is often riddled with words that put ourselves and others down.

Our words are clues to our thoughts and feelings. We can learn about ourselves by listening to ourselves. We can begin to let go of negative attitudes and behaviors by letting go of negative words.

I will seek to eliminate negative words from my thought and speech.

Patience

We choose to be either patient or impatient many times each day. We have to wait for people, computers, traffic lights, and the preparation of food. Impatience doesn't make us feel better. It only makes us nervous, angry, and unable to enjoy ourselves.

We learn patience by practicing. When we drive up to a flashing light at a railroad crossing, instead of turning around and finding another route, we can wait. We can turn off the engine, relax, think, pray, look around, or listen to music. We can watch as children do, wondering what's inside the boxcars, noticing signs of where they've been or where they're going. A quiet moment like this won't spoil our day or destroy our schedule. It just might help us, refresh us, calm us down, and remind us to be patient.

I let go of impatience and enjoy each moment.

"I Was Wrong"

Admitting when we are wrong may be difficult. We may feel we should always know the right thing to do or say. We may believe others only like or respect us when we are right.

We may feel so bad about making mistakes that we deny them or blame them on others. But this only compounds our errors, filling us with guilt, anger, and fear of exposure.

Saying, "I was wrong," can be like having a dental cavity filled. We know it may hurt a bit, but it will save us much greater, longer-lasting pain. After we've done it a few times, it becomes less painful, because we know it's going to make us feel better. Admitting when we're wrong keeps us from accumulating guilt, anger, denial, and fear. We don't have to be perfect. We just have to accept that we're not.

I admit when I'm wrong, and I accept my imperfection.

Obsession

Being obsessed means to be troubled, haunted, or excessively preoccupied by an idea or thought. This is the way codependents often think about other people and their problems.

Obviously, being obsessed with someone else makes it nearly impossible to think clearly about other things. Obsessions keep us from focusing on ourselves.

All of our worrying, imagining, manipulating, and trying to change others just doesn't work. We can let go of our obsessions by accepting our powerlessness and concentrating our thoughts and energy on our own responsibilities.

We have the power to let go of obsessive thoughts and let God take care of the things we can't change. Then we can turn our attention to improving ourselves and our lives.

I let go of obsessive thoughts.

Judgments

We have found that letting go of controlling attitudes and behaviors requires letting go of our judgments of others. But we may still judge events, situations, and circumstances. We may still become upset by, and try to control, "bad" things that happen.

William Shakespeare wrote, "There is nothing either good or bad, but thinking makes it so." When we judge the weather or our luck as bad, we can only respond with fear, anger, or despair. When we accept the things we can't control, we are free to think more clearly about whatever we need to do.

Most of the circumstances we judge as "bad" are merely changes, requiring us to adjust our thinking and behavior. When we let go of self-pity over the changes we face, we can stop judging them and accept them with serenity.

I accept the things I can't control, without judgments.

Good-bye to the Past

The past is gone, except in our minds. When we dwell on past hurts, mistakes, or even joys, we can't focus on the present. No amount of thinking or worrying can change the past or recapture it and bring it into the present.

We can now say a loving good-bye to the past, thanking all of our experiences for the lessons they brought us. Then we can concentrate on what is here and now. We can fully experience each new moment as it comes. We can also give our full attention to each new lesson as it is presented to us.

As we turn our minds to each present moment, we find ourselves recognizing the continuum of life. Who we are now is a result of past lessons learned. We don't need to remember the experiences that taught us the lessons, only the lessons themselves.

Today is the only place in time that exists. I release my past and everyone in it.

Prayer and Meditation

In working our program, we learn the value of prayer and meditation. But old controlling habits can creep into even this area of our lives.

In prayer we may compile a list of requests, believing we know what's best. In meditation, we may have difficulty letting go of our thoughts and hearing God's voice.

Our constant thoughts about what we want may block our communication with God. We need to open our hearts, minds, and ears to the messages coming to us.

In prayer, we can simply ask our Higher Power for help in every area of our lives, and for the knowledge of what's best for us. In meditation, we can quiet our thoughts and open ourselves up to receiving God's messages. When we let go of our desire for control, we can use prayer and meditation to develop our relationship with God.

I let go of controlling thoughts and open myself to hearing God's message.

Physical Release

Letting go of negative emotions may be helped by physical exertion. We may customarily scream at people, slam doors, or break dishes when we are upset. But these actions are harmful and only make us feel worse.

There are many nondestructive ways to burn off uncomfortable feelings. Brisk walking, running, swimming; playing tennis, basketball, racquetball, or handball; scrubbing floors, washing windows or a car; or punching pillows—all can help release negative emotions without hurting anyone.

We carry a lot of our emotions in our bodies, and physical release can help clear them. We may need physical activity the most when we are sore and feel like it the least. The soreness may be caused by pent-up feelings. The best way to soothe those aches and pains may be to get moving.

Physical exercise will make me feel better, even when I don't feel like it.

Magical Thinking

Many of us grew up with stories of people's problems and dangers being removed by magical force. Cinderella had a Fairy Godmother, Aladdin had a lamp, and Sleeping Beauty had three Fairy Godmothers and a Handsome Prince!

In real life, nothing is ever solved by wishing on a star. We may believe we have given up magical thinking, but we may expect a new job, spouse, car, town, baby, or home to solve all our problems. We may believe we'd live happily ever after if only someone or something in our lives would change.

Magical thinking places all the responsibility for our happiness outside ourselves, as though some future circumstance will provide perfect and everlasting joy.

Letting go of magical thinking requires solving our own problems. Our reward is peace and contentment, here and now.

I let go of magical thinking and accept responsibility for myself.

Perfectionism ☆

Many of us are never satisfied, particularly with ourselves. If we score a base hit, it should be a home run. If we get a part in a play, it should be the lead. If we get the lead, it should be a better play, theater, director. . .

We never let ourselves enjoy the good things in our lives when we only want *great* things. The trouble is, we can't think of anything we actually attain as great. There's always something better.

Our perfectionism robs us of the ability to appreciate every step along the path of our personal development and spiritual evolution.

One thing we can be sure of is that none of us will reach perfection in this life. Remembering this certainty can help us enjoy the pleasures and accomplishments of each day.

I release my pefectionism and open myself to all the things to be enjoyed in my life today.

Recreation

In the past, we may have felt so responsible for other people's lives and happiness that we forgot how to relax and enjoy ourselves.

We have been learning how to use our time and energy better. We have started doing more things for ourselves and saying no when we need to. But we still need time for recreation. No one is a bottomless well of energy and effort. We need to rest and re-fuel. Recreation means to *re-create*, to revive, refresh, replenish.

If we aren't used to fun and play, it may feel strange at first to let go of our inhibitions for a while. But running, walking, swimming, playing sports or games, flying a kite, singing and dancing, or just having a good laugh, can help us perform all of the rest of our activities better.

I will regularly take time for recreation.

Control

We may still be unaware of all the ways we try to control. Caring can quickly become caretaking. Participation can easily slip into manipulation. Concern can become obsession before we realize it.

We need to ask ourselves every day, in every situation and relationship, if we are slipping into controlling attitudes or behaviors. Every night we can review the day for signs of worry; obsession; caretaking; manipulation; helplessness or dependency; domination; coercion; provoking guilt or anger; and giving unwanted advice.

As we catch ourselves slipping into these old practices, we can turn the situation, relationship, or event over to our Higher Power. We can trust it will be taken care of without our interference.

Every day I watch for controlling behavior and let it go immediately.

Fear

As codependents, we may have developed many fears. We may be afraid of other people, emotions, change, independence, relationships, responsibility, or intimacy. Letting go may seem impossible.

But as we move along our spiritual pathway, we learn we can choose to grow and recover in spite of our fears.

Taking care of ourselves requires facing fear, doing things we haven't done before, and letting go of familiar attitudes and behaviors. We can ask our Higher Power for help—not necessarily to remove our fears, but rather for strength and courage to keep pressing on regardless of them.

We all have fears. The choice we need to make is whether or not to let them stop us from working toward greater health and happiness. It's up to us.

I accept my fears and move forward in spite of them.

Not a Victim

If past relationships were harmful to us, as children or adults, we may see ourselves as victims. We may allow others to abuse us in various ways, feeling on some level that it's appropriate.

But we can move beyond this self-defeating behavior. Our self-image lives in our minds, and we have the power to change it. We are not victims unless we see ourselves that way. Even if we were unable to protect ourselves from abuse in the past, that doesn't make us victims now.

Letting go of our distorted self-image will change our behavior. We will see ourselves as whole and responsible. We will accept the things we can't change, and change the things we can.

I am not a victim.

Seasons

In nature, each season gives way gracefully to the next. Summer ends in a brilliant blaze of fall color. Winter departs, leaving rain and melting snow to nourish the re-awakening earth. The changes of season reflect the ever-changing nature of all life.

In our own lives, we may kick, scream, and fight changes that come our way. We may feel threatened by the loss of old familiar attitudes, behaviors, and relationships. We dare not hope the changes will be for the best.

But just as we have learned to trust the changing seasons, we can develop faith in our changing lives. We can expect that whatever our Higher Power sends our way can be for our highest good. We can believe that difficulties will pass and each change will bring us further along our spiritual path.

I trust that the changes in my life are necessary and good for me.

A Moment to Reflect
Meditations for Codependents

Letting Go
Setting Boundaries
Accepting Ourselves
Living Our Own Lives